Read-About® Math

Divide It Up!

By Tonya Leslie

Consultant
Ari Ginsburg
Math Curriculum Specialist

Children's Press®
A Division of Scholastic Inc.
New York   Toronto   London   Auckland   Sydney
Mexico City   New Delhi   Hong Kong
Danbury, Connecticut

Designer: Herman Adler Design
Photo Researcher: Caroline Anderson
The photo on the cover shows how three cookies divided by three children
equals one cookie for each child.

Library of Congress Cataloging-in-Publication Data

Leslie, Tonya.
  Divide it up! / by Tonya Leslie ; consultant, Ari Ginsburg.
    p. cm. — (Rookie read-about math)
  Includes index.
  ISBN 0-516-25261-5 (lib. bdg.)   0-516-25362-X (pbk.)
  1. Division—Juvenile literature. I. Ginsburg, Ari. II. Title. III. Series.
  QA115.L466 2005
  513.2'14—dc22   2005004537

1 2 3 4 5 6 7 8 9 10 R 14 13 12 11 10 09 08 07 06 05

In school you need to share.
How do you share things?

You divide them up!

How do you divide something? You split it up into parts.

When you divide something equally, everyone gets a fair share.

This is a symbol. A symbol is something that stands for something else.

This symbol means divide.

When you see this symbol, it means you have to divide something into equal parts.

Here is how you divide.
First, you have to know
how many things you have.

Then, you have to know
how many parts you need
to divide those things into.

4 cookies ÷ 4 children =

1 cookie for each child

9

Can you make sure
everyone gets a fair
share? Try it and see!

Look at these two pears.
Two friends want to
eat them.

How would you divide
the pears?

First, write down the
number of pears.

2 pears

Then, write down the number of friends who want pears.

2 friends

Two pears divided by two
friends equals one pear
for each friend.

Each friend gets a fair
share of pear!

When you divide a number
of things into the same
number of parts, the
answer is always one.

2 pears ÷ 2 friends =
1 pear for each friend

Let's try another one.
Look at these four crayons.

Two friends want to draw
with them. How would
you divide the crayons?

First, write down the number of crayons.

4 crayons

Then, write down the number
of people who need crayons.

2 friends

Four crayons divided by two friends means each friend gets two crayons!

4 crayons ÷ 2 friends =
2 crayons for each friend

Let's try a harder one.
Look at these six
toy animals.

Three friends want to
play with them. How
would you divide the
toy animals equally?

First, write down the number of toy animals.

Then, write down the number of friends who want to play with the animals.

Six toy animals divided by three students means each student gets two toy animals.

6 toy animals ÷ 3 friends =
2 toy animals for each friend

You can divide! You made
sure everyone got a fair share.

Now it gets tricky.
There is one teacher.

There are six students.
Each student wants a hug.
Can everyone get a hug?

Yes!

One great teacher equals
lots of hugs for everybody!

Words You Know

cookies

crayons

divide

friends

30

pears

teacher

toy animals

Index

About the Author

Tonya Leslie is a teacher and writer who lives in New York City.
She likes reading, dancing, and good food.

Photo Credits